HANDEL

The King shall rejoice

1727

Coronation Anthem for SATB & orchestra

Piano accompaniment arranged from the score
with additional accompaniments by Edouard Silas

Order No: NOV 07 0131

NOVELLO PUBLISHING LIMITED

THE KING SHALL REJOICE.

No. 1. CHORUS.—"THE KING SHALL REJOICE."

A
Soprano.
The King shall re- joice, the King shall re - joice in Thy strength, O Lord,
Alto.
The King shall re- joice, the King shall re - joice in Thy strength, O Lord,
Tenor.
The King shall re-joice, the King shall re - joice in Thy strength, O Lord,
Bass.
The King shall re- joice, the King shall re -joice in Thy strength, O Lord,
A

The King shall re - joice, shall re - joice, . . .
The King shall re - joice, shall re - joice, . . .
The King shall re - joice, shall re - joice, . . .
The King shall re - joice, shall re - joice . . .
tr
tr
tr

. . . . shall re - joice in Thy strength, O
. . . . shall re - joice in Thy strength, O
. . . . shall re - joice in Thy strength, O
. . . . in Thy strength, O
Lord, the King shall re - joice, ... the King shall re - joice in Thy strength, O
Lord, the King shall re - joice, ... the King shall re - joice in Thy strength, O
Lord, the King shall re - joice, ... the King shall re - joice in Thy strength, O
Lord, the King shall re - joice, ... the King shall re - joice in Thy strength, O

B
Lord, the King shall re-joice,
Lord, the King shall re-joice, the King shall re-
Lord, the King shall re-joice, the King shall re-
Lord, the King shall re-joice, the King shall re-
B

shall rejoice, shall re-joice, shall re-joice in Thy strength, O
-joice, shall re-joice in Thy strength, O
-joice, shall rejoice, shall re-joice, shall rejoice, shall re-joice in Thy strength, O
-joice, in Thy strength, O

C
Lord, the King shall re-joice in Thy strength, O Lord, in Thy strength, O
Lord, the King shall re-joice in Thy strength, O Lord, in Thy strength, O
Lord, the King shall re-joice in Thy strength, O Lord, in Thy strength, O
Lord, the King shall re-joice in Thy strength, O Lord, in Thy strength, O
tr
C

Lord, the King shall re - joice, ... the King shall re
Lord, the King shall re - joice, ... the King shall re -
Lord, the King shall re - joice, ... the King shall re -
Lord, the King shall re - joice, ... the King shall re -
tr

- joice in Thy strength, O Lord,
the King shall re - joice,
- joice in Thy strength, O Lord,
the King shall re - joice,
- joice in Thy strength, O Lord,
the King shall re - joice,
- joice in Thy strength, O Lord,
the King shall re - joice,
tr

the King shall re - joice in Thy strength, O Lord!
the King shall re - joice in Thy strength, O Lord!
the King shall re - joice in Thy strength, O Lord!
the King shall re - joice in Thy strength, O Lord!
tr

No. 2. QUARTET OR CHORUS.—"EXCEEDING GLAD SHALL HE BE."

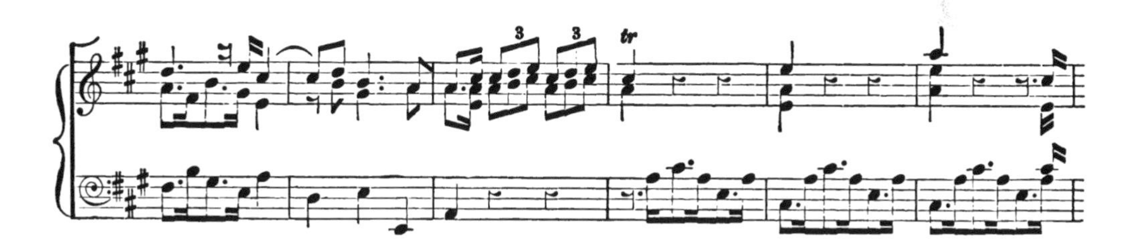

ex - ceed - ing glad, glad, ex - ceed - ing glad shall he
ex - ceed - ing glad, ex - ceed - ing glad, glad shall he
ex - ceed - ing glad, ex - ceed - ing glad, glad shall he
ex - ceed - ing glad, glad, ex - ceed - ing glad shall he
R.
E
be
be of Thy sal - va
be
be of Thy sal - va - tion,
E
of Thy sal - va - tion,
tion,
of Thy sal - va - tion,
of Thy sal - va - tion, of Thy sal -

of Thy sal - va - - - - - - - - - - tion.
of Thy sal - va - - tion, of Thy sal - va - tion.
of Thy sal - va - - - - - - - - tion.
- va - - - - - - - - - - - tion, Thy sal - va - tion.
F
Ex - ceed - ing
Ex- ceed- ing glad shall he be,
Ex- ceed- ing glad shall he be,
Ex-ceed - ing
glad shall he be, ex - ceed-ing glad shall he be
ex - ceed- ing glad, ex - ceed- ing glad shall he
ex - ceed- ing glad, glad shall he be,
glad shall he be, ex - ceed-ing glad, ex-ceed- ing glad shall he

of Thy sal - va - - - - - - - - - - - -
be of Thy sal - va - - - - - tion,
of Thy sal -
be, ex - ceed-ing glad, ex - ceed-ing glad,
G
- - - - - - - - - tion,
of Thy sal - va - - - - - tion, of Thy sal -
- va - - - - - - tion,
of Thy sal - va - - - - - tion, of Thy sal - va - - -
G
of Thy sal - va - - - - - - - tion, of
- va - - - - - - - - - - - tion, of
of Thy sal - va - - - - - - - - tion, of . . .
- - - - - - - - - - - - - - - tion, of

Thy sal - va -
Thy sal - va -
Thy sal - va -
Thy sal - va -
tion. Ex - ceed - ing glad shall he be,
tion. Ex - ceed - ing glad shall he be,
tion. Ex - ceed - ing glad shall he be,
tion. Ex - ceed - ing glad shall he be,
H
ex - ceed - ing glad, ex - ceed - ing glad shall he
of Thy sal - va - tion, ex - ceed - ing
of Thy sal - va -
ex - ceed - ing glad, ex - ceed - ing glad shall he
H

be of Thy sal - - - - va - - -
glad of Thy sal - - - - va - - -
- tion, of Thy sal - - - - va - - -
be of Thy sal - - - - va - - -
3
3

- - - - - - tion, of Thy sal - va - tion.
- - - - - - tion, of Thy sal - va - tion.
- - - - - - tion, of Thy sal - va - tion.
- - - - - - tion, of Thy sal - va - tion.
B.

3

p
f
3

No. 3. Chorus.—"GLORY AND GREAT WORSHIP."

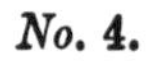

No. 4. CHORUS.—"THOU HAST PREVENTED HIM."

- ness, with the bless - - - - - - - - ings of . . good- ness, . .
him with the bless - - - - - - - - - - - - ings of . .
him,
. . . with the bless - ings of good-ness, Thou, Thou hast pre-vent - ed
good - ness, . . with the bless - ings of good - ness, Thou hast pre-vent - ed
Thou hast pre - vent - - - - ed him
I
Thou hast pre - vent - - - - - - ed
him with the bless - ings . . of good - -
him with the bless - - - - ings of good- ness,
with the bless - - - - - - - - - ings of good - - - - - - -
I

him with the bless - - - - - - - - - - -
- ness, with the bless - ings, with the
Thou, Thou hast pre - vent - ed him,
- ness, with the bless - ings of good - - ness,
- - - - - - - - - - - ings of . . . good - ness,
bless - ings of good - ness, with the blessings of
Thou hast pre - vent - ed him with the blessings of
Thou hast pre - vent - - - - - ed him with the blessings of
K
and hast set a crown of pure
good - ness, and hast set a crown of pure
good - - ness, and hast set a crown of pure
good-ness, and hast set a crown of pure
K

gold up - on his head,
gold up - on his head, Thou, Thou hast pre - vent - ed him,
gold up - on his head, Thou, Thou hast
gold up - on his head, Thou, Thou hast
ff
and hast set a crown of pure
and hast set a crown of pure
pre-vent - ed him, and hast set a crown of pure
pre-vent - ed him, and hast set a crown of pure
gold up - on his head, Thou hast pre - vent -
gold up - on his head,
gold up - on his head,
gold up - on his head,
mf.

ed him
mf
Thou, Thou hast pre-vent-ed him with the bless -
mf
Thou, Thou hast pre-vent-ed him with the blessings of good-ness,
with the bless - ings of
ings of good-ness,
tr
with the bless - ings of good -
M
ff
good-ness, and hast set a crown of pure
ff
and hast set a crown of pure
ff
ness, and hast set a crown of pure
ff
and hast set a crown of pure
M
ff

gold, and hast set . . a crown of pure gold . . .
gold, and hath set . . a crown of pure gold . . .
gold, and hast set a crown of pure gold . . .
gold, and hast set . . a crown of pure gold . . .
. . up-on his head.
up - on his head.
up - on his head.
up - on his head.
dim.

No. 5.
CHORUS.—"ALLELUJAH."
Allegro.
SOPRANO.
ALTO.
TENOR.
BASS.
PIANO.
♩=112.
Al - le-lu - jah, ... Al -
Al - le - lu - jah, Al-le - lu - jah, Al-le - lu - jah, Al - le - lu -
Al - le -
Al - le - lu - jah, . . Al - le - lu - jah, Al - le -
- le - lu - jah,
Al - le -
- jah, Al - le - lu - jah, . . . Al - le - lu - jah, . . Al - le -
- lu - jah, Al-le - lu - jah, Al - le - lu - jah, ... Al - le -

- lu - jah, Al - le - lu - jah, Al - le - lu - jah, Al - le - lu - jah, Al - le - lu -
- lu - jah, Al - le - lu - jah, ... Al - le - lu - jah, Al - le - lu -
- lu - jah, Al - le - lu - jah, Al - le - lu - jah, Al - le - lu - jah, Al - le - lu -
- lu - jah, Al - le - lu - jah, Al - le - lu - jah, Al - le - lu - jah, ...
- jah, Al - le - lu - jah, Al - le - lu - jah, Al - le - lu - jah, . .
- jah, Al - le - lu - jah, Al - le - lu - jah, Al - le - lu - jah, . .
- jah, Al - le - lu - jah, Al - le - lu - jah, Al - le - lu - jah . .
. . . . Al - le - lu - jah, . .
N
Al - le - lu - jah, ... Al - le - lu - jah, . .
Al - le - lu - jah, Al - le - lu - jah, . . Al - le - lu - jah, . .
Al - le - lu - jah, Al - le - lu - jah, Al - le - lu - jah,
Al - le - lu - jah, Al - le - lu - jah, . . Al - le - lu - jah, . .
N

Al - le - lu - jah, ... Al - le - lu - jah, Al - le - -
Al - le - lu - jah, Al - le - lu - jah, . . Al - le - lu - jah, Al - le - lu -
Al - le - lu - jah, Al - le - lu - jah, . . Al - le - lu - jah, Al - le - -
Al - le - lu - jah, Al - le - lu - jah, . . Al - le - lu - jah, Al - le - lu -
- - - - lu - jah, Al - le - - - - lu - jah, Al - le - lu - jah, Al - le - lu -
- jah, Al - le - lu - jah, Al - le - - - - lu - jah, ... Al - le - lu -
- - - - - lu - jah, Al - le - - - - lu - jah,
- jah, Al - le - lu - jah, Al - le - - - - lu - jah,
L. H.
- jah, ...
- jah, ... Al - le - lu - jah, ...
Al - le - lu - jah, ...
Al - le - lu - jah, ...

Al - le - lu - jah, Al -
Al - le - lu - jah, Al - le - lu - jah, Al - le -
Al - le - lu - jah, Al - le - lu - jah, Al - le - lu - jah,
Al - le - lu - jah, Al - le - lu - jah, Al - le - lu - jah,
tr
- le - lu - jah, Al - le-lu - jah, Al - le - lu - jah,
- lu - jah, Al - le - lu - jah, Al-le - lu - jah, Al - le - lu - jah, Al le-lu -
Al - le - lu - jah, Al - le - lu - jah, Al -
Al - le-lu - jah,
R.H.
P
Al-le-lu - jah, Al - le - lu -
- jah, Al-le-lu-jah, Al-le-lu-jah, Al - le - lu -
- le - lu - jah, Al-le-lu-jah, Al-le-lu-jah, Al - le - lu -
Al-le-lu-jah, Al-le-lu-jah, Al - le - lu -
P

jah, . .
Al - le - lu - jah,
jah, . .
Al - le - lu-jah,
Al- le - lu-jah,
Al - le - lu - jah,
jah, . .
Al - le - lu-jah,
Al- le - lu-jah,
jah, . .
Al - le - lu - jah,
Q
Al-le - lu - jah,
Al-le - lu - jah,
Al - le - lu - jah,
Al - le - lu - jah,
Q
ff
Al - le - lu - jah, Al - le - lu - jah, Al - le - lu - jah, Al - le - lu -
Al - le - lu - jah, Al - le - lu - jah, Al - le - lu -
Al - le - lu - jah, Al - le - lu - jah, Al - le - lu - jah, Al - le - lu -
Al - le - lu - jah, Al - le - lu - jah, Al - le - lu - jah, Al - le - lu -

Published by Novello Publishing Limited
Printed in Great Britain By Caligraving Limited, Thetford, Norfolk.

EARLY CHORAL MUSIC

BONONCINI, Antonio
ed Peter Smith
STABAT MATER
For SATB soli, SATB chorus, strings and organ

BONONCINI, Giovanni
ed Anthony Ford
WHEN SAUL WAS KING
For SAT soli, SATB chorus, strings and organ continuo, with optional parts for two oboes and bassoon

GABRIELI, Giovanni
ed Denis Stevens
IN ECCLESIIS
For SATB soli, SATB chorus, instruments and organ

LASSUS, Orlandus
ed Clive Wearing
STABAT MATER
For unaccompanied double choir (SSAT, ATTB)

MONTEVERDI, Claudio
ed John Steele
BEATUS VIR
For SSATTB chorus, instruments and organ continuo

PALESTRINA, da Giovanni
ed W Barclay Squire
STABAT MATER
For unaccompanied double choir (SATB, SATB)

RIGATTI, Giovanni Antonio
ed Jerome Roche
CONFITEBOR TIBI
For SSAATTB chorus, instruments and organ continuo

SCARLATTI, Alessandro
ed John Steele
AUDI FILIA
For SSA soli, SSATB chorus, instruments, string orchestra and organ
ed John Steele
DIXIT DOMINUS
For SATB soli, SATB chorus, strings and organ continuo
ed John Steele
ST CECILIA MASS
For SSATB soli, SATB chorus, strings and organ continuo

VALLS, Francisco
MISSA SCALA ARETINA
For 11 voices in 3 choirs (SAT, SSAT, SATB), orchestra with organ continuo

VARIOUS
TEN RENAISSANCE DIALOGUES
For unaccompanied mixed voices by Lassus, Gabrieli, Morley and others